First edition for the United States and Canada published
in 2010 by Barron's Educational Series, Inc.

First edition of *I can make a difference*
first published in 2010 by Wayland, a division of Hachette Children's Books

All inquiries should be addressed to:
Barron's Educational Series, Inc.
250 Wireless Boulevard
Hauppauge, NY 11788
www.barronseduc.com

Library of Congress Control No.: 2010925446

ISBN-13: 978-0-7641-4516-2
ISBN-10: 0-7641-4516-9

Printed in China
9 8 7 6 5 4 3 2 1

Manufactured by: Shenzhen Wing King Tong Paper Products Co. Ltd., Shenzhen, Guangdong, China.
May 2010

I Can Make a Difference

A FIRST LOOK AT SETTING A GOOD EXAMPLE

PAT THOMAS
ILLUSTRATED BY LESLEY HARKER

BARRON'S

Every person in the world is a teacher.
Even you. Did you know that?

Every day we teach each other
how to do things. And we learn
from each other too—even if
we don't always know it.

When we watch someone, and copy the things they do,
we are learning from their example.

If we copy people who set a good example,
by behaving well and treating others with kindness,
that is how we will learn to behave.

And if we copy people who
behave badly, and treat others unkindly,
that is how we will learn to behave, too.

The best way to set a good example is to treat others the way you want them to treat you...

...and to take care of your family, your friends, and your home in the way you would like others to take care of them.

Some people set good examples
for us all in the work that
they do.

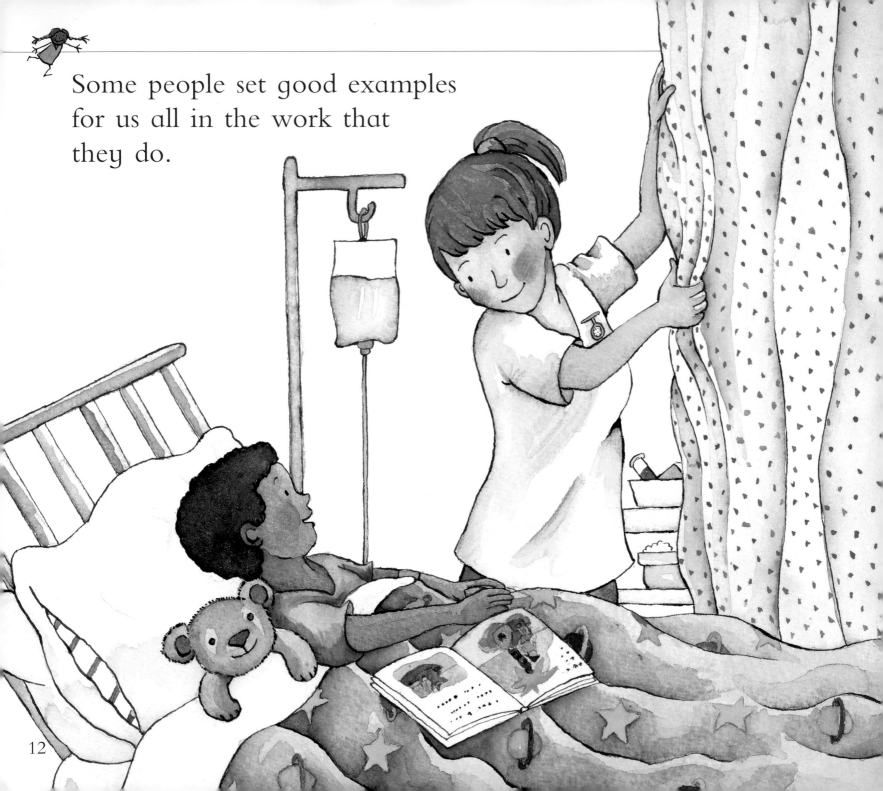

But all of us can find ways to set
a good example every day.

You can set a good example by saying "please" and "thank you," never making fun of others, and offering to help...

... or by protecting those who are smaller or weaker than you, and helping to keep things clean and neat.

You can help by carrying the heavy things, not throwing garbage on the ground, congratulating the winning team, or reading to a sick friend.

What about you?

Can you think of some people who do jobs that set a good example for us all? Can you think of some ways your parents set a good example to follow? Can you think of some ways that you might set a good example?

It's not just about taking care
of others, though.

You can also set
a good example by
taking good care of yourself.

Nobody's perfect all the time.

We all make mistakes and
every once in a while we all do
things and say things that aren't very nice.

When that happens, saying "I'm sorry"—and meaning it by not repeating what you did—is another way to set a good example.

Sometimes you might wonder why
it is important to set a good example,
especially when you see other
people who never do.

You might also wonder if the way one person acts can really make a difference. Lots of adults wonder this too.

What about you?

Can you think of some times when you have seen other people setting a poor example? What happened? How did that make you feel?

Every person on earth has a choice about how they behave and how they treat others.

By setting a good example, and doing your best, you are teaching other people to act the same way.

And if those
people copy you,
then everyone they
know will also learn
this important lesson.

When everyone tries their best to behave well, it makes our families, our classrooms, and our communities nicer places to be.

It makes working and playing together easier
and more enjoyable.

Most people who choose to be kind and polite to others want to make the world a better place.

It's like planting seeds in a garden.
The more you plant, the more beautiful
the garden will become.

HOW TO USE THIS BOOK

It has been said that there are only three things a parent needs to know about raising considerate, responsible, well-mannered children: Example, example, example. Who children become is deeply influenced by the example set by those who raise them. So, as a first step, it's worth considering what kind of example we want to set, what qualities we would like our children to have when they grow up, and examining how we as parents and caregivers can communicate these values.

Consider how you can model courtesy—those small acts of consideration that show respect for the child, from which the child learns to give that courtesy back to you. Simple good examples any parent or caregiver can set involve: using kind words, helping when you can, sharing, listening to what others have to say, being honest and truthful, thinking before you speak and act, practicing good manners, controlling your temper, thinking about the feelings of others, and applying the principles of fairness at home and at work.

In addition, provide context where you can. Children often have no idea why we do what we do, so talk about what you are doing and why. If we take soup to a sick friend, or if we work on a community project, explain why you think it's important to be helpful and/or take some responsibility in the community. This can help our children understand our reasoning and relate our activities to their own behavior.

Try taking a step-by-step approach. Start with the "magic words" such as "please" and "thank you." Gradually add more examples such as "you're welcome" and "pardon me?" and "may I...?" As children get a little older, you can work on actions like picking up toys, table manners, looking after siblings, taking care of pets, etc.

Remember to compliment your children when they behave well. Saying "Holding the door for that woman carrying all those heavy bags was very polite" or "I saw how well you got along with everyone at sports day, well done" will send a more positive message than constantly reprimanding them when they are not behaving well.

Young children are old enough to understand rules and the consequences of breaking those rules. When defining what is and isn't acceptable behavior, parents and teachers alike can help by setting fair rules with clear explanations for why these have been set.

You can't always get it right. We all lose our tempers, say things we're sorry for, or are not always as kind as we would like to be. Admit your failures, apologize where you need to, and move on with a view to how you might act differently next time. Set an example of admitting your own failings and improving your own behavior and your child will be encouraged to do the same.

Schools provide ample opportunities for children to practice a whole range of skills. Setting a good example can be found in citizenship lessons which emphasize the importance of recognizing similarities as well as valuing differences between people, helping one another, and providing service to the larger school community.

BOOKS TO READ

I'll Do It!: Learning About Responsibility
Brian Moses (Wayland, 1998)

Teaching Citizenship Through Traditional Tales
Sue Ellis, Deirdre Grogan (Scholastic, 2003)

The Bad Good Manners Book
Babette Cole (Hamish Hamilton Ltd, 1995)

The Children's Book of Heroes
William J. Bennett (Simon & Schuster, 1997)

Where the Wild Things Are
Maurice Sendak (Harper Collins, 1988)

Why Should I Share?
Claire Llewellyn (Barron's, 2005)

Why Should I Recycle?
Jen Green (Barron's, 2005)

RESOURCES FOR ADULTS

Chicken Soup for the Soul: Character-Building Stories to Read with Kids
Jack Canfield (HGI, 2007)

How to Talk So Kids Will Listen and Listen So Kids Will Talk (How to Help Your Child)
Adele Faber, Elain Mazlish (Piccadilly Press Ltd, 2001)

Teaching Your Children Values
Lind and Richard Eyre (Fireside, 1993)